Terms and Conditions

LEGAL NOTICE

The Publisher has strived to be as accurate and complete as possible in the creation of this report, notwithstanding the fact that he does not warrant or represent at any time that the contents within are accurate due to the rapidly changing nature of the Internet.

While all attempts have been made to verify information provided in this publication, the Publisher assumes no responsibility for errors, omissions, or contrary interpretation of the subject matter herein. Any perceived slights of specific persons, peoples, or organizations are unintentional.

In practical advice books, like anything else in life, there are no guarantees of income made. Readers are cautioned to reply on their own judgment about their individual circumstances to act accordingly.

This book is not intended for use as a source of legal, business, accounting or financial advice. All readers are advised to seek services of competent professionals in legal, business, accounting and finance fields.

You are encouraged to print this book for easy reading.

Table Of Contents

Forward

Chapter 1:
Getting Automated: A Dream Come True

Chapter 2: AboutColdCalling

Chapter 3:
GoodMarketing

Chapter 4:
AdditionalTools

Chapter 5:
Site Name And Instructing The Team

Chapter 6:
ViralMarketing

Chapter 7:
SEOBasics

Chapter 8:
UsingE-mail

WrappingUp

Foreword

Why is the Net pepping up network marketing? In the fast paced time and era of the data age, individuals get ahead in life not by working hard solely – they have to work smart!

The 3 most fruitful industries in the world are:
(1) Information Technology
(2) Telecommunications
(3) Network Marketing

What does the Net have to offer?
Conceive of:
- Net Order Processing
- Autoresponders
- Video Conferencing
- Lead Capture Pages
- Rich Media Advertising
- E-mail Blasting
- And more...

These are illustrations of a few tools on the Net that may be utilized to your advantage in your network marketing business. I'll explain that more in the subsequent chapters about how each of those tools may greatly profit your network marketing efforts.

Preparing For Wave 5

How Any Network Marketer Can Utilize The Google Era To Skyrocket Their Network Marketing Profits.

Chapter 1:
Getting Automated: A Dream Come True

Synopsis

In net marketing, individuals always discuss leverage. But what do we leverage on? Individuals. Since the technological revolution, individuals would leverage their efforts on other individuals. Individuals from the past up to now: worker bees, serfs, laborers, employees, referrals, associates or downline. Everybody has merely twenty-four hours and they utilize others time in exchange for something else.

Auto-Pilot

Did you realize that now you are able to take this leveraging element one step further utilizing the Net? All because of the mere e-mail. Note how a mere e-mail may make a sale for you without making a telephone call, looking for your acquaintances, or driving all the way to the mall to buy your prospect a drink.

An autoresponder is a tool that sends out a pre-written e-mail or script, tailor-made toward the prospect's details for him to be pitched about your merchandise or your opportunity. Without getting out of your seat, you are able to assemble a web page and anybody who wants more info can enter his name, e-mail address and telephone number. You are able to get these leads by arranging a lead capture page. These pages may be published in the form of a sales letter. They'll do the selling for you day in and day out even while you're logging Z's.

Individuals who buy your business or product online will be able to utilize the product at once if it is a digital product. If it's a physical product, the network marketing company commonly sets up shipping or delivery.

If the lead doesn't buy the product but rather enters his particulars in the webpage, the autoresponder will send off a series of e-mails to the lead for 2 purposes: supplying additional info and follow up. They'll continue receiving these e-mails till they either purchase something from you or request the system to remove them off their subscriber base.

Do you recognize how mighty utilizing the Net is in helping your network marketing business develop leaps and bounds? Think. Most individuals will only be able to meet a determined number of leads in a day (traveling takes time and individuals will only see you at their convenience). On the Net, your potential clientele is roughly 1000000000000!

And do you recognize that as all the sales pitching, prospecting, and follow through may be machine-driven by a few easy, pre-written e-mails, it will help save you so much time, you'll be giddy!
"This is too great to be real... What's the catch?"

Well, your networking business doesn't go on automatic pilot automatically. You'll still have to interact with your downline (they're still your obligation after all), guide them and most significant of all, becoming their friend.

No long term business may ever be launched without building relationships. Individuals build relationships with their buyers (then they'll get repeat sales), partners (so their vested interest will forever be there), and resellers.

Using the Net essentially takes the heavy load off your back. It's like plowing the field with a tractor rather than utilizing horses.

Chapter 2:

About Cold Calling

Synopsis

Does your company or your upline demand you to recruit like crazy? Does calling guarantee that you'll sponsor new individuals? If your business instructs you to call 50-100 individuals a day or approach strangers, getting their numbers and then pitching them your opportunity one by one, and, if this scheme is working out fine for you and your group, then do not alter what you're doing. But if you're seeking something else then we ought to explore why cold calling strangers isn't good.

The Reasons

(1) You can't sell. Even if you could, not all of your team can sell like you.

(2) Individuals don't like being sold to! Do you like house-to-house salesmen? (Even if you are a house-to-house salesman, you won't like them coming to your home).

(3) Cold calling strangers make the one on the receiving end to invoke their defenses, as they don't know you and they can't see your face.

(4) If you're a stranger, they may not purchase from you, as they'll think you're attempting to get into their pocket.

(5) Cold calling demands posture, which is something the lead, has the right to say no to and control the flow of the conversation.

If those reasons are not adequate, consider your telephone bill. Do you expect all your downlines to accomplish success this way? It's true that not all will purchase from you even after you've done the consummate presentation. We all understand that 'some will, some won't, so what?' But what if we may filter those who won't out, and center on those who will?

Don't you believe it will save you lots of time and revenue? Wouldn't you preferably work with those who are willing instead of waste your time with those who aren't?

The Net is designed more for the customer's mindset. Why do I say that? The Net provides its users privacy. They commonly surf

whatever they wish by themselves and they may buy their own goods without the need to meet with others like in a marketplace. Take the example of house-to-house salesmen or salesmen who go table-to-table. They approach you and you commonly wouldn't want to purchase from them. You'd be thinking, "Why are you selling me something? If I wanted what you're marketing, I'd have purchased it already!" See the difference between purchasing and selling? Individuals love to purchase. They don't like to be sold to.

On the Net, don't center on pitching the opportunity. Instead, pitch info on how to or conjure up the curiosity of the buyer. Individuals will seek something to purchase so they may resolve their own issues. By understanding this central point, you'll see how to funnel targeted traffic or great quality leads for your opportunity.

After some time, they'll request more info or look in deeper on how to solve their issues. How do you work this out?

Take these 2 scenarios for example:

Scenario 1

Distributor: Hi, I'm from x company. We specialize in wellness supplements. Do you value your wellness in general? Lead: naturally I do.

Distributor: Excellent! Now our range of products help to resolve hypertension, slim down, relieve constipation, etc. Do you have any specific area of concern in these health regions?

Lead: Err... yes, sort of but not truly a big concern. (What? Do you wish me to imply that I am ill or something? I do have these issues but I don't believe I prefer to share these with you as I don't truly know you.)

Distributor: Here is our catalog. You'll be able to find it will resolve all sorts of health issues. My contact number is here and you may likewise check out their site. You may truly make lots of cash in the health industry with this fantastic opportunity!

Lead: all right. Thanks. I'll give you a call once I view it. I really gotta go now.

Notice: The lead is being sold to. I'm not saying the distributor isn't doing a great job. Perhaps the lead might be having a bad day or he had an argument with his mate.
Now, let's turn the tables on him.

Scenario 2

Here the distributor has a little ad in the paper where it discusses free of charge info on wellness issues and displays the site address. He may even place an ad in Google. Following the lead looks up the ad and follows the link. He views the info online and the lead capture page requests him to type in his e-mail address so he may get more 'expert' advice.

The autoresponder provides him an e-mail with details or reports of wellness in general and the lead becomes more intrigued. The lead becomes schooled. Two things may occur here if he's intrigued.

He decides to buy a little, detailed health manual to comprehend more about his body or he decides to buy a trial pack of the real product.

The lead gives a call to the distributor who put up the site and asks him questions, as he's intrigued. The distributor then shares the advantages of the product.

The sale is done and he may even be interested in the opportunity as he's so happy with the product.

Notice: The lead is really the right purchaser but he just doesn't know that this product is for him when he's being sold to. By selling to him, the opportunity to gain a fresh downline or buyer may be lost forever.

The other conceivable thing that may happen is that he's financially not able at the moment and didn't have adequate time to digest all the info. The autoresponder does the follow-up, presenting him a series of e-mails to continually update the lead. Afterwards he may either purchase the product or contact the distributor for additional details.

See how mighty tools may be in network marketing? And the best thing of all, you won't have to pester leads like a beggar! You'll be more like an authority that's sharing info instead of selling things. This technique is really rejection free as the leads come to you!

Chapter 3:
Good Marketing

Synopsis

A lot of the time, individuals advertise with the wrong sort of ads to bring in more prospects to sign up. They advertise full or part time work with a great income and a great company.

The candidate shows up anticipating an interview, but you show the plan instead. The candidate would either get angry that he has been duped into a network marketing opportunity or be baffled about the whole deal. It gets even more horrible when he has to come out with his own cash to qualify for the 'job'.

Ads And A Sales Page

Individuals are not stupid. Departed are the days of bluffing leads into opportunity meetings.

If you use a short ad explaining its network marketing, that probably won't work either. The prospect will think, must be one of those networking things once more. If the prospect is already in a company, he'll think, "I'm already in one. So what? Telephone so you may sell me a different opportunity?" Not effective advertising also.

If you use the age old ad that the company runs itself...not good either. If you tell your readers that no true work is involved, they'll do just that – no work. You'll exhaust yourself with these guys and give yourselves even more work as you're pulling in all the lazy free loaders out there.

So what are the standards for a great marketing ad?

When a lead telephones, some attempt to explain everything on the telephone in an attempt to sell their opportunity or product. This is a huge no-no as the lead will get confused and he has the option to say no and close the door. The goal is to acquire their contact number or e-mail! The goal is to get them to view your sales letter online.

If your company doesn't have a great online system, then I advocate you writing your own sales letter which will lead to the data you're trying to share. A great sales letter will sell for you every minute and you may tailor make its message to bring the lead to make an emotional decision (as many buyers purchase on impulse or based on an emotional conclusion).

Your ad material ought to be structured to lead the prospect in small stages. From acquiring the contact info (by giving away free info), to educating the lead about the product (discovering their need or pain), and then recommending the product thru the site. Then afterwards upsell the purchase to provide more value.

Here is a simple illustration for a health ad:
Sick of sleepiness?
Log-in to (site) for a free of charge wellness report about how to better your energy!

Your sales letter must hold material that will take the lead on an emotional journey. This is more of an art than a skill as your sales letter has to hold the prospect's attention long enough till he reads to the end of the page and arrives at a decision or else you'll have no fresh sign ups.

The central point to remember is that in network marketing, there are 1000000s of distributors in the same business. What distinguishes you from other distributors? Why should the lead join you rather than others? This is where the sales letter enters. Your sales letter will distinguish you from the rest.

As a guideline, your sales letter must have relevant happy and write as much relevant info required. Commonly, longer sales letters are better than shorter ones as you're giving info away freely and you wish the prospects to make an intelligent decision. Remember this central point as it will make or break your business. You're not selling merchandise or opportunities; you're selling resolutions to an issue or helping other people to develop or prevent loss.

Here are 4 things to remember:

(1) Why ought or do I wish to purchase your merchandise in the 1st place? Bring out his pain or concern. If you can't even answer this query, your chance of procuring the sale is zilch.

(2) Even if I do wish to purchase it – why should I purchase it from you, and not somebody else? Here you might outline a few of the advantages of joining the company, but most significant of all, you ought to never forget to market you. Individuals join you and not the company. You have to show him that you've the right credentials.

(3) All right, so if I do wish to purchase it from you, why should I pay you the price you are asking? You have to justify why the buyer should pay you the price you're asking then you'll have a great chance of a sign up. Attempt to show him that actually what you're asking for is much less than its real value.

(4) Why should I purchase it today? Is there a great reason for your prospect to purchase the product today rather than later? Chances are if he doesn't purchase from you today, he will never purchase it later. One way is to his prompt response is to provide him with bonuses or gratis training materials.

Once you've answered all these questions, you'll have a high chance to acquire a new buyer or a new distributor. Then you may follow through with him off-line, establish the relationship with him, and train him.

Chapter 4:
Additional Tools

Synopsis

There are a lot of tools available on the Net that will enhance your network marketing business. For instance, you are able to utilize live video conferencing to send your message across to your leads or downline.

One really useful tool that may be utilized for prospecting is rich media advertisement. Another is newsletters. How does it work?

Helpful Tools

Essentially, this is a more advanced way of utilizing the Net to 'show the plan'. They engage more of the 5 senses instead of centering on utilizing text and graphics in the sales letter solely.

It exhibits a video or animation that will take you through as though you're on a journey. The video commonly has sounds or somebody that will vocally (pre-recorded) explain the advantage of the product or opportunity. Music is likewise utilized to give the prospect a really dynamic feeling about the business.

There are commonly choices that will strategically funnel the prospect to arrive at a decision toward purchasing the product or joining the business. The most beneficial thing about this tool is that it has custom features which will allow your newly signed on distributors or downline to duplicate the system effortlessly! A great example would be after they sign on, they may send the video to their own prospects but tailor-make the system by changing the name of the prospect or distributor during the presentation (a few of them even pronounce your name during the presentation).

Envisage, you won't need to learn how to be an ace salesman or teach that to all your downline. Simply learn to utilize the system and you may easily repeat results in your team!
How may you use forums and e-zines to your advantage? You may easily sign on and create Yahoo! Groups and get your members to come online for get togethers and discussions.

A few of the uses of forums will include:
(1) Announcement of the next meeting at which topic.

(2) Info about the company.

(3) Welcoming a fresh member when he signs on to the forum (this will provide him confidence and a feeling of belonging to the team).

(4) Declaring the new achievers (thus giving enormous encouragement).

(5) Downloading of company booklets, merchandising tools, training material.

(6) Photographs uploaded that might showcase the new autos, recent achiever's vacation trips, team rallies and team member profiles.

There are so many ways this may keep your team together. It's up to your creativity how you wish to establish your business. E-zines are likewise really great as they will update all the distributors on the events the company is having or the launch of a bran-new product.

You may even utilize the computer to instruct and train individuals how to calculate the compensation plan. A few compensation plans are really complex and you don't need to be a math mastermind to calculate them because computer tools are simple to utilize and will help individuals solve complex issues really fast.

Chapter 5:
Site Name And Instructing The Team

Synopsis

It's really crucial to own your own domain name. It gives you a way to better your professionalism leaps and bounds and it costs way less than launching an office.

Domain names are you net presence and individuals will see that through your site.

Domain names are really essential because it's like branding yourself and giving you self-ownership of your business. Many individuals will see you more professionally if you've a site like this (all links here are strictly for illustrational purposes)

http://www.aboutNetworking.com

Suppose if your domain name is something like this

http://www.networking.blogspot.com

Your leads will think you're not professional enough as you're riding on the name of other larger domains and it gives the impression that you're not really self-branding (or taking your business earnestly enough).

Important Points

Great domain names likewise enhances visibility online through search engine results, sets you apart from rivalry, leaves a firm impression in the minds of your leads and get the most individuals to come to your web site.

The same applies for e-mail. Which would you judge as a more professional person?

networking@yahoo.com
OR
yourname@networking.com

If both would approach me to link up with their opportunity, I would sooner join the second one. The distinction is sort of obvious who's more professional.

One more significant point to think about is the affiliate links. If your company provides you an affiliate link like http://www.mlmcompanyname.com/?reF924 or www.mlmchance.com/yourname, you're leaving a lot of cash on the table.

How come? You're losing business as individuals like to delete the link at the end as they wish to visit the primary site or see the 'pure' site as it is. Occasionally individuals find it too tedious and simply delete it, as they know the info will still be on the primary site anyhow.

The other issue is that today individuals aren't so good at remembering numbers or they might spell names wrong occasionally (that's how come they record all the names and numbers on their hand phone and utilize speed dial).

If I'm advertising my site, I'd wish my leads to get the site typed correctly the 1st time. How do you remedy this? URL redirect. You may check the info on Google to set up these services. URL redirect will let the prospect type in one site and send it to the affiliate links rather than having them type the whole thing in.

Individuals are commonly petrified of change. When fresh technology pops up individuals dread becoming obsolete themselves. Let's face it; there are individuals who refuse to learn something new. Regrettably, change is inevitable just like death and taxes (or else individuals would still be riding horses rather than using autos today).

Many individuals have an e-mail address and you don't have to be a skilful Net marketer, web-designer or programmer to utilize this. The most significant thing to do in order to duplicate Net tools downline (which will help your group get ahead) is to accent the price saving and expanded signs on of using the tools.

Most individuals buy leads or pump their hard earned cash into advertising and drive from place to place spending cash on gasoline and raking up a huge telephone bill. A few of them are already spending so much and they haven't even made their first check in their industry!

Net advertising, e-mails and forums cost very little to almost zip and you don't have to drive or make many calls. If someone is serious

about building a long term network marketing business, there's no way he would refuse the chance to bring down all these expenses and get the chance to enroll more downline!

Moreover, it's simpler to duplicate a net tool than to teach all distributors to walk and speak like the leader. Truth be told, not everybody may speak very well, so why not let the Net do all the 'talking' for you?

Chapter 6:
Viral Marketing

Synopsis

Viral marketing is no more a fresh concept. This means of advertising has produced valuable effects even for big, well established companies, who have discovered it exceedingly advantageous as a factor of their marketing campaigns.

Hotmail led off from nowhere and advanced to 1000000s of users in just under two years with the force of viral marketing.

If you would like to learn how to rule the force of this excellent marketing tool, than you truly need to continue reading! The viral marketing tips that you require to develop your campaigns and make them a success are defined here and moreover, with viral marketing you've nothing to lose but only to gain. If you don't utilize viral marketing, you're only injuring yourself. You are able to bet that the guys vying with you for the same internet traffic are utilizing it! Don't get lost in the bunch!

Learn these useful keys to success. It's not as difficult as you believe to get your viral marketing crusade off the ground.

Buzz

Today individuals are sharing info, collaborating on issues of interest, and networking on the Net in ways not previously imaginable. In Viral, most common ways are video, photos, music, games and likewise even presentations. These tools deviate depending on the idea in the campaign. For example, if you wish to spread a video, it's ideal for video-sharing sites like YouTube. But if we're talking about a multi-platform campaign, the utilization of social media especially social networks (Facebook, Twitter …etc.) and blogs is the better.

The most useful element of any successful viral marketing is to first be as well-educated about your product as you are about yourself. Each product/service has a little story to tell, utilize this for your own benefit. If it doesn't have one you may make one up, but be sure it has a little likable or exciting event that will interest individuals in your viral campaign.

Promoting is all about snatching their attention, yet upholding the 'mystery' element. While your story has to have the features of something both interesting and exciting, it too has to stay a story with viral potential. To accomplish this, you have to keep your product/service a secret and let individuals get involved. You're not simply making an obscure sales talk – you're forging an entire campaign around the principle of your product. Because of this, your story can't resonate as being too promotional. Hard sell content will turn individuals off.

When you've a viral campaign that has been successful, you should not let this opportunity go. As a matter of fact, it's always a great idea to use the success you experienced with a viral marketing campaign.

What is the most beneficial way to achieve continuing a viral campaign?

Shortly following the success of the first one, you ought to have a follow-up effort and target the same individuals who helped you circulate the first one. Individuals like seeing "behind the scenes" video recording; if you've such video available, utilize it to build expectations of approaching campaigns or products. This sort of thing may be a vital element in establishing your campaigns in the future, so attempt to recapture the interest that you'd initially aroused. And it's simply another great way to keep inhabit wanting for more after your initial success.

The greatest tip is to tell you that you have to make certain your campaign is unequalled. Most individuals react to being surprised, shocked or exhilarated. If you give the audience something that delights them, they'll of course spread your content around. Don't resort to predictable techniques and content; an unforeseen approach interests individuals.

It's a fact that individuals don't like to be sold, and thus they've become really immune to any sort of advertising. Advertising is commonly deemed self-centered: a way to get your cash into my pocket. You'll have to present yourself in an unequalled way, so make certain that your viral marketing campaign is something altogether innovative and unique. Most of all, you must never ever come across as being ho-hum. Reach inside of you and take out all the stops, every possible piece of creativity you have, and wow them!

Chapter 7:
SEO Basics

Synopsis

As many of us already understand, Google is rated by many as the number 1 search engine in the world. We personally understand that our sites get about 90% of their search engine traffic direct from Google searches.

Becoming indexed by Google may be a pain, but acquiring highly placed rankings for particular keywords seems to be the nut that not a lot of web developers without SEO (search engine optimization) experience or seo training may crack.

We're going to provide info on the basics of SEO techniques — many of which we utilize daily to optimize our sites and stay ahead of our rivals.

Optimize

Picking out the correct keywords to base your site optimization around is a crucial opening move. General or generic keywords are commonly not the better approach, and occasionally it's better to be a bit more specific and center on niche keywords relating to your product or service.

For instance, let's discuss a WYSIWYG HTML editing component that is used in browser-based applications. The issue is, there are many WYSIWYG HTML editors, but how may we get ours to appear in Google's top 10 rankings? Well, let's see. Attempting to optimize for the keyword "HTML" solely would be a hard job, as it's too common. There are HTML editors, HTML tutorials, HTML content, etc.

We have to be more particular, which implies:
1. Targeting a more appropriate market that's seeking a content editing solution
2. Vying with fewer sites targeting the same keywords
3. Optimizing for keywords that individuals really utilize when doing searches

Targeting an appropriate market will depend upon your site, as well as the products and services you provide. Attempt to be particular with your keywords, and remember that individuals no longer utilize single keyword search phrases – the normal search phrase bears 3-5 related words. For instance, if you're optimizing for a web development site and you're located in Phoenix, AZ. utilize keywords like "web development Phoenix" or "web development services AZ".

To discover how many sites are competing with your keywords — either purposely or not — merely do a search on Google and note down how many results are yielded. In our case, for "net html editor", we're vying with 8,080,000 sites. The more sites that are vying for your keywords, the more difficult it will be to get on the front page.

As a rough rule of thumb, attempt to optimize each page on your site for a different search phrase. Every search phrase should contain 2 to 3 extremely targeted keywords.

2 of the most crucial elements in Google's ranking are your domain name and title tag. For instance, a domain name like: http://www.web-development-az.com will generally become ranked higher than http://www.companyname.com, assuming that they had identical keywords and page substance.

For a few of us, keywords in the DNS look too unprofessional, and we've already registered our domain, so it's too late to switch. An alternative — and likewise a valuable tactic — is to add your keywords into the names of your pages, like http://www.companyname.com/net-development-services.html

Your title tag is every bit as crucial as your domain name. Utilizing keywords in your title tag may improve your Google ranking significantly. Attempting to accomplish a balance of professionalism with keyword density in the title tag nonetheless is occasionally a bit harder.

Going back to our illustration of a net development company earlier, a great title tag would be: <title>"Company name provides pro affordable net development services in Phoenix, AZ." </title>

Commonly, the closer to the front of your title tag the keywords are placed, the more beneficial.

<H1> tags appear to have been devalued by style sheets these days, and are not utilized as frequently as they used to be.

The Google ranking algorithmic rule prescribes that if you're utilizing a <H1> tag, then the text in between this tag must be more crucial than the material on the rest of the page. Here's a fast illustration:

<H1>Google sees this text as more crucial</H1>
<p>... than this</p>

By default, H1 tags aren't the prettiest in terms of formatting, so utilizing a CSS style to overrule the default look is commonly a great idea: H1 { color: blue; font-family: Arial; font-size: 14px }

Dispersing keywords throughout your page material may also better your sites keyword density. Keyword density merely means the ratio of optimized keywords to the rest of the material on your page. It's commonly expressed as a percent, and ought to be between 7% and 10% for every page on your site.

Don't exaggerate the keyword density, however, but don't neglect it either. A great illustration would be:

Previously: Company name supplies net design and site management services to our customers.

Following: Company name supplies net development services to the Phoenix region in AZ

Note how we utilize the keywords more efficiently the 2nd time around?

And this leads us to the hardest part of the Google SEO process — back-links. Back links are sites that link directly to your site. The common principal is the more back links you enjoy, the greater your pages will be ranked, as your site must be great if so many other sites are linking back.

If you run a net development company, then putting in a simple link on the bottom of each of your client's sites, like:<a href=http://www.yoursite.com>Net development by Company Name</a>... (With your customers permission naturally) may help boost your back links, which will help boost your ranking location in searches.

Posting your site to dmoz.org, Yahoo! and other directories is likewise a crucial step to better the number of sites linking back to yours. Do remember though, that arranging back links takes time. I'd recommend emailing 5-10 sites each and every day to petition back-links or partnership links (holding in mind that the sites contacted ought to be relevant but not competitive) for example. – If you sell cocoa, partnering with a company that sells Hershey's might just be a great idea. Inside a few weeks, you ought to have a good hundred or so sites merrily linking back to yours!

Google may be one hard search engine to crack. Hopefully, though, in this chapter we've provided you with adequate basic tips to get moving optimizing your site.

Chapter 8:
Using E-mail

Synopsis

Today e-mail continues to be the most profitable and affordable way to get hold of prospects and buyers. A study discovered 78% of business e-mail marketers and 69% of consumer e-mail marketers still believe that e-mail marketing is effective, and its affect continues to grow.

However, what does all this mean to you, the industrious small business owner? It means that your rivals and businesses whose products you utilize daily (like your bank, cell phone provider and accountant) are all utilizing e-mail marketing to their benefit.

Mailing

Regardless what industry you're in, there are a lot of ways you may utilize e-mail marketing to draw in new leads and turn them into life long evangelists and repeat customers.

Here's a couple of reasons why you ought to be utilizing e-mail marketing to compliment your additional marketing actions:

It's exceedingly effective. E-mail marketing works to establish a trusted bond between you and your leads and buyers. Once you've earned a leads trust it gets to be much easier to sell to them. As a matter of fact, you don't even have to apply the "hard sell" as in their brain you're more like a trusted acquaintance with merchandise and services they require, instead of a faceless company.

It's measurable. How do you assess the success of a television or radio ad blitz? Guesswork would be most individual's response. With e-mail marketing you may see precisely how many individuals have opened your e-mail and which links they clicked (if you've a site). You simply can't get this sort of measurable campaign info from any former communication medium.

It's low-cost. Utilizing an e-mail marketing tool costs merely a few cents to send an e-mail to a lead or existing buyer and you may do it yourself. Because individuals have voluntarily subscribed to your e-mail list, they're more receptive to your content than any other medium, including television, radio and print.

It's amusing. Truly! It's difficult to describe the feeling you get once you send off an e-mail to your subscriber list and you see –

immediately – how many individuals are opening your e-mail and which links they're clicking on. It's really a liberating experience, which may become quite habit-forming.

Wrapping Up

There is a formula that goes in network marketing:

$$\text{Speed} + \text{size of it} = \text{momentum}$$

The Net gives us prospecting speed. Reaching out to 1000000s of targeted audiences instead of holding an opportunity meeting and many couldn't show up due to time constraints or being too busy.

Automated signs on and registration processing helps a lot, instead of carrying a stack of forms driving up and down to the central office submitting them.

This is the age of info. It is not about scarcely working hard any longer. The most crucial thing to remember is that the Net may automate all the tools for you, but at the end of the day, it's you who must switch it on.

Here is a story that goes:

There was a wood cutter who went to a shop searching for an axe. The storekeeper rather tried selling him a chainsaw and outlined all the advantages of saving time and work and chopping more trees. He even gave him a cash back guarantee if it didn't work.

The wood cutter smiled with mirth and purchased the chainsaw. Three days later, he came back to the store. He was cut and bruised as if he returned from war. He said the chain saw didn't work and was totally exhausted. He wanted his cash back.

The storekeeper then agreed to refund his cash but before he did that, he pulled the string on the chain saw to test it out. After he switched it on, the wood cutter shouted, "What is that sound?"

The moral of the tale is you must learn to turn on the tools. Then you'll be at the closest thing to Networking nirvana.

www.ingramcontent.com/pod-product-compliance
Lightning Source LLC
Chambersburg PA
CBHW030539220526
45463CB00007B/2909